JN079177

せいしょのほんやくをかんせいして
てんにかえったビードせんせい

ビードさん
Mr Bede

Mr Bede who translated the Gospel of
St John in his deathbed

ぶん）はまじま　びん
え）　みのわ　まりこ

Bin Hamajima
Mariko Minowa

22世紀アート

本書を読んでくださる皆様へ

　私は、ずっと聖書に関わり、特に研究の一環として、聖書翻訳の研究をしてきました。そして一つ一つの翻訳の背後に、素晴らしいエピソードがあることを感じていました。聖書そのものの素晴らしさはもちろんですが、それを民衆に与えるために努力した人々、中には、そのために自分の命さえ捧げた人たちがいます。それらの人たちに関する本を数冊執筆、また翻訳してきました。それで、このような素晴らしい人たちのことを子供たちにもぜひ知ってほしいと思いました。絵本であればそれを読んでくださるご両親にも同時に知っていただくことができます。そして、この企画をしました。前期１０冊、後期１０冊ほどの絵本シリーズにしたいと願っています。

　絵を描いてくださる方をずっと求めていましたが、幸い箕輪まり子様という素晴らしい方を紹介していただきました。私と思いを共有していただき、素晴らしい絵を描いていただきました。私の思いを超えた綺麗で温かい絵です。きっと子供たちばかりでなく、大人の人たちにも多くの感動を与えてくれると信じています。何よりも、このシリーズが、読む人を感動させ、神様に栄光をお帰しすることが、私たちの最も希望するところです。

浜島　敏

Dear readers,

I have been involved with the Bible for a very long time. In particular, I have been studying Bible translations as part of my research. And I have got the impression that there is a wonderful story behind each and every translation. The Bible itself is of course a wonderful book, but there are also a great many people who have worked very hard to bring it to the masses, some of whom have even given up their lives for this purpose. I have written and translated several books on such figures, and I wanted children to know about these wonderful people as well. I realised that writing a picture book would be a great way to have the parents learn their lives as well, as they read the story to thier children.

I had been looking for someone to do the illustrations for a long time, and I was fortunate enough to be introduced to a wonderful person, Ms Mariko Minowa. She shared my feelings and created wonderful illustrations. Her illustrations are warmer and more beautiful than I could have ever hoped for. I am convinced that they have the power to move and impress both children and adults alike. Our greatest hope is that this series will inspire those who read it and bring glory to God.

Bin Hamajima

イギリスのきたのほうに
ニューカースルという
おおきなまちがあります

そのちかくの
ジャローというちいさなまちに
ふるいきょうかいがあります

In the north of England

there is a large city called

Newcastle-upon-Tyne.

And near the city, in the small town

of Jarrow,

there stands an old church.

ビードさんは

ちいさいときに　このきょうかいの

しゅうどういんに　はいり

それから　ずっと

かみさまのことや　せいしょの

べんきょうを　していました

ビードさんは、おべんきょうが

だいすきでした

When he was a child,

Mr Bede entered

the monastery attached to this church.

Since then,

he learned about God and the Bible.

Mr Bede loved to study the Word of God.

たくさんべんきょうをして

みんなにかみさまの

おはなしをする　せんせいになりました

ビードさんは　かみさまの

おしごとをすることが

とても　すきでした

ビードせんせいと　よばれ

みんなから　そんけいされていました

He learned a lot and

became a teacher

and taught about God to

monks in the monastery.

Mr Bede loved working for God.

He was called "Venerable Bede",

and was loved and

respected by everyone.

それから、ビードさんは
イギリスに　どのように
キリストきょうが　つたえられ
ひろまっていったのかを　しらべ
とても　たいせつな
ほんを　かきました

Then, Mr Bede wrote a big

and very important history book:

The Church History of

the English People.

In the book, he wrote when and

how Christianity was

brought to Britain,

and how it spread quick

and wide in the country.

ビードせんせいは　としをとって

びょうきになり　あまり

むりな　しごとが　できなく　なりました

けれども　ビードせんせいは

さいごに　どうしても

しておきたいしごとが　ありました

それは　せいしょが

みんなの　わかる　ことばで

よめるようにすると　いうことでした

とうじは、むずかしいがいこくごの

せいしょしか　ありませんでした

Now Mr Bede grew old (62 years old)

and became ill,

so he was not able to do hard works any more.

However, there was one last thing

he really wanted to do.

He wanted to translate the Bible into English,

common language of the people,

so that anyone who wanted could

read the word of God.

Most of the Bibles at that time

were copied in Latin,

and there were no English translations.

ビードせんせいは

いすに　すわっています

となりには　わかい　おでしさんが

ペンを　てに もって　すわっています

ビードせんせいが

せいしょの　ことばを

すこしずつ　えいごに　なおしています

それを　おでしさんが

いっしょうけんめいに

かいているのです

Mr Bede is sitting in his chair.

A young man is sitting facing him

with a pen in his hand.

Mr Bede is slowly translating

the words

and phrases of the Bible into English.

And the young man writes

it down with care.

ビードせんせいは

ベッドによこになっています

びょうきで　くるしそうです

「せんせい　これいじょうは

たいへんですから

このへんでやめて

どうぞ　おやすみください」

「いや　いや　まだ　だいじょうぶです

これは　とても　たいせつなしごとだから

がんばって　つづけなさい」

Mr Bede is lying on his bed.

He's very ill now.

He has a pain in his legs.

"Sir, this is too much for you.

Please stop here,

and have some rest."

"No. This is a very important work.

Sharpen your pen

and continue the work.

それから　また
なんにちか　のちのことです
「せんせい　あと
すこしだけに　なりました」

「よろしい　それでは
がんばって　かいてください」

And a few days later.

"Sir, there are only a few more

sentences left."

"Good. Keep on the good work!"

「せんせい、　とうとう　おわりました」

「よかったですね　それでは

わたしを　おこしてください

まどのほうを　むいて　かみさまに

かんしゃの　おいのりを　しましょう」

" Sir, you've finally finished."

"Very good. Now,

help me up toward the window.

And together, let us thank God for

His help.

ビードせんせいはかみさまに

さんびの　うたを　うたって

かみさまにむかえられて

てんごくにたびだちました

Mr Bede sang a song of

praise to God,

and breathed his last.

He was received by God in heaven.

保護者の皆様、教会学校の先生方へ

　イギリスの東北にニューカースルという町がありますが、その郊外に、ジャローというところがあります。タイン川の支流ドン川に面した町で、ビード（673～735）は、7歳のときに、近くのウェアマスという場所の修道院に入り、後にジャローの修道院に移り、ここで一生を終わった人です。彼の家柄などについては、あまり知られていません。7世紀から8世紀にかけて、活躍した人ですが、730年に『英国民教会史』という大変大きな本を書きました。そして、英国に、どのようにキリスト教が伝えられたか、また、その後、どのように広がっていったのかを詳しく書き記しました。イギリスには、最初にアイルランドを経由して、ケルト系のキリスト教がまず入り、スコットランドから北部に盛んに宣教活動が行われましたが、後にローマ系のキリスト教が南から入り、カンタベリーに本拠を置き、北に向かって宣教をしました。両者がぶつかることもありましたが、やがて、ローマ派が勝利し全土に広がりました。ビードの本は、ローマ派の正当性を述べたものであります。これは、今でも、当時のキリスト教に限らず、イギリスの初期の歴史を知る第一資料としてとても価値のあるものとされています。

　今、歴史の本は、世界中で「西暦」を基本にして書かれていますが、西暦、すなわち、キリスト暦を土台に系統的な歴史を書いたのはビードが最初だと言われています。彼には、たくさんの弟子がいましたが、彼らは、ヨーロッパ大陸に出かけ、たくさんの仕事をしました。特にドイツのカロリング・ルネッサンスの立て役者であるアルクイヌスは彼の孫弟子です。

　ビードは死の直前まで、聖書の翻訳をしていたと彼の弟子の一人が伝えています。非常に感動的な物語ですが、ヨハネ伝の口述を行っていて、かなり病気で苦しい中、それを最後までやり終えて、天に帰ったということです。残念ながら、それがどんなものだったのか、今残ってはおりませんので、わかりませんが、教会では一般にラテン語が使われていましたので、それをラテン語のわからない人たちのために、英語に翻訳した意味はとても大きいと思います。

　ビードが一生のほとんどを過ごしたジャローの教会は、今も訪れる人が多いですが、教会にはビードが座った椅子があり、大きなビードの木像が教会内中央に吊るされています。

To Parents and Sunday School Teachers

In the northeast of England, there is a city called Newcastle, on the outskirts of which lies a town called Jarrow facing the River Don, a tributary of the River Tyne. At the age of seven, Bede (673-735) entered a monastery in Wearmouth. Later, he moved to the monastery in Jarrow, where he lived the rest of his life. Not much is known about his family lineage. He was active in the 7th and 8th centuries, and in 730, he wrote an extremely large book titled *Ecclesiastical History of the English People*. He wrote in detail about how Christianity was introduced into England and how it spread afterward. Celtic Christianity first entered Britain by way of Ireland, and missionaries were active from Scotland all the way to the northern reaches of the country. Later, however, Roman Christianity entered from the south and began to spread northward from its centre in Canterbury. The two occasionally clashed, but Roman Christianity soon prevailed and spread throughout the entire country. Bede's book details the legitimacy of Roman Christianity. To this day, it is still valued as a primary source of information on not only the Christianity of the time but also on the early history of England.

History books throughout the world are now written based on the Western calendar, but Bede is said to be the first person to ever compile a systematic history based on the Western – in other words, the Christian – calendar. He had numerous disciples who travelled to the European mainland for a broad range of undertakings. Of particular note is Alcuin, a disciple of one of Bede's disciples, who went on to become a leading figure of Carolingian renaissance.

According to one of his disciples, Bede was working to translate the Bible until the moment of his death. It is a very touching story. He dictated the Gospel of John, and despite suffering from extreme pain, he pushed through to the end before finally returning to Heaven.

To this day, the church in Jarrow where Bede spent most of his life still receives many visitors. Inside the church, visitors can see the chair that Bede sat in as well as large wooden statute of Bede hanging in the centre of the church.

【著者】

浜島敏（はまじま　びん）、愛知県出身、明治学院大学大学院修了。

四国学院大学名誉教授。言語学、聖書翻訳研究。

会員：善通寺バプテスト教会、国際景教研究会、日本国際ギデオン協会ほか。

【イラストレーター】

箕輪まり子（みのわ　まりこ）、東京都出身、

Instagram：https://instagram.com/waawa.maricoool?igshid
=OGQ5ZDc2ODk2ZA==

会員：日本ホーリネス教団池の上キリスト教会。

【Author】

HAMAJIMA, Bin, M.A./ Th.D.; born in Aichi; Professor Emeritus of Shikoku Gakuin University; member: Zentsuji Baptist Church; Society of Jingjian Religion, Gideons International.

【Illustrator】

MINOWA, Mariko, born in Tokyo,

Instagram：https://instagram.com/waawa.maricoool?igshid
=OGQ5ZDc2ODk2ZA==

Ikenoue Christian Church.

せいしょのほんやくをかんせいして
てんにかえったビードせんせい

ビードさん

2023年6月30日発行	文	はまじま びん
	絵	みのわ まりこ
	発行者	向 田 翔 一

発行所　　株式会社 22 世紀アート
　　　　　〒103-0007
　　　　　東京都中央区日本橋浜町 3-23-1-5F
　　　　　電話　03-5941-9774
　　　　　Email: info@22art.net　ホームページ：www.22art.net

発売元　　株式会社日興企画
　　　　　〒104-0032
　　　　　東京都中央区八丁堀 4-11-10 第 2SS ビル 6F
　　　　　電話　03-6262-8127
　　　　　Email: support@nikko-kikaku.com
　　　　　ホームページ：https://nikko-kikaku.com/

印刷
製本　　　株式会社 PUBFUN

ISBN : 978-4-88877-223-5
© はまじま びん、みのわ まりこ 2023, printed in Japan
本書は著作権上の保護を受けています。
本書の一部または全部について無断で複写することを禁じます。
乱丁・落丁本はお取り替えいたします。